To _____

From _____

For Couples in Love

Published by Garborg's Heart 'n Home, Inc.
P. O. Box 20132
Bloomington, MN 55420

SPCN 5-5044-0064-3

Two human loves make one divine.

—ELIZABETH BARRETT BROWNING

JANUARY 1

*I wish I could tell you the day,
the hour, the minute my love for you
became real. I only know it seems
I've loved you forever.*

—ANONYMOUS

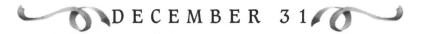

DECEMBER 31

*May the Lord bring you
into an even deeper understanding of
the love of God and of the patience
that comes from Christ.*

—2 THESSALONIANS 3:5 TLB

 JANUARY 2

*My greatest happiness lies
in the intertwining of our dreams,
hopes, hearts, and minds.
With all my heart I love you.*

—MARY SHAFER

DECEMBER 30

*Love decreases when
it ceases to increase.*

—VICOMTE DE CHATEAUBRIAND

JANUARY 3

Hail! wedded love,
Perpetual fountain of domestic sweets!

—JOHN MILTON

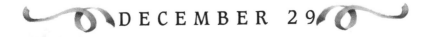

DECEMBER 29

*To love for the sake of being loved
is human, but to love for the sake
of loving is angelic.*

—DE LAMARTINE

JANUARY 4

*To love is to place our happiness
in the happiness of another.*

—GOTTFRIED WILHELM VON LUBREITZ

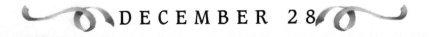 DECEMBER 28

*Love the Lord your God
with all your heart and with all your
soul and with all your strength.*

—DEUTERONOMY 6:5 NIV

 JANUARY 5

*Love can hope
where reason would despair.*

—LORD LYTTELTON

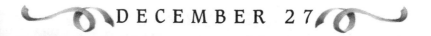 DECEMBER 27

*Love sought is good,
but given unsought is better.*

—SHAKESPEARE

JANUARY 6

*Marriage is not a thing of nature
but a gift of God.*

—MARTIN LUTHER

DECEMBER 26

*If there is anything better
than to be loved, it is loving.*

—ANONYMOUS

JANUARY 7

*Christmas is a time of the heart,
not just a date. Its meaning transcends
time. Jesus was born to love us and
fill our lives with himself.*

—ANONYMOUS

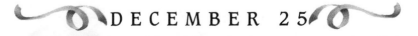

DECEMBER 25

You were united to your wife by the Lord. In God's wise plan, when you married, the two of you became one person in his sight.

MALACHI 2:15 TLB

JANUARY 8

The most vivid memories of
Christmases past are usually not of gifts
given or received, but of the spirit of love,
the special warmth of Christmas worship,
the cherished little habits of the home.

—LOIS RAND

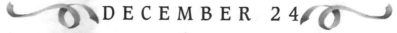

DECEMBER 24

The Kiss—
Something made of nothing,
tasting very sweet.

—M. E. BUELI

JANUARY 9

Outward beauties are but the props and scaffolds on which we build our love...which, now made perfect, stands without those supports.

—SIR JOHN DENHAM

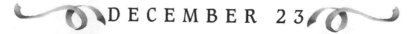

DECEMBER 23

*The hearts that love will
Know never winter's frost and chill.
Summer's warmth is in them still.*

—EBEN EUGENE REXFORD

 JANUARY 10

Thou hast no faults,
or I no faults can spy;
Thou art all beauty,
or all blindness I.

—C. CODRINGTON

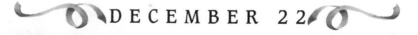

DECEMBER 22

*May they who love you be like
the sun when it rises in its strength.*

—JUDGES 5:31 NIV

JANUARY 11

Love—*thoughts of tenderness, tried in temptation, strengthened by distress, unmoved by absence, and yet, more than all, untired by time.*

—LORD BYRON

DECEMBER 21

*They do not love that
do not show their love.*

—HEYWOOD

JANUARY 12

Let all that you do be done in love.

—1 CORINTHIANS 16:14 RSV

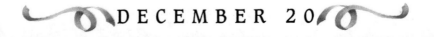

DECEMBER 20

I like not only to be loved,
but to be told I am loved.

—GEORGE ELIOT

JANUARY 13

As soon as you cannot keep anything from a woman, you love her.

—ANONYMOUS

DECEMBER 19

As for me and my house,
we will serve the Lord.

—JOSHUA 24:15 KJV

JANUARY 14

*Pains of love be sweeter far
Than all other pleasures are.*

—JOHN DRYDEN

DECEMBER 18

Love and you shall be loved.

—RALPH WALDO EMERSON

JANUARY 15

*Marriage is a union in which joys
are multiplied and troubles divided.*

—ANONYMOUS

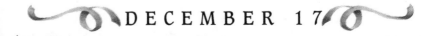

DECEMBER 17

*The supreme happiness of life
is the conviction of being loved
for yourself, or more correctly,
being loved in spite of yourself.*

—VICTOR HUGO

JANUARY 16

*Tis love alone can hearts unlock:
Who knows the word, he needs not knock.*

—RICHARD CRASHAW

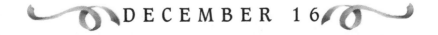

DECEMBER 16

*Let the wife of your youth
be your companion; be bathed in her
love, and her love will continually
wrap you around.*

—PROVERBS 5:18,19 NEB

JANUARY 17

Love is an ever-fixed mark that looks on tempests and is never shaken.

—SHAKESPEARE

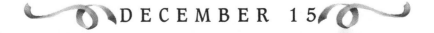

DECEMBER 15

*Love is the only passion
which includes in its dreams the
happiness of someone else.*

—KARR

 JANUARY 18

For since a man and his wife are
now one, a man is really doing himself
a favor and loving himself
when he loves his wife!

—EPHESIANS 5:28 TLB

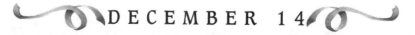

DECEMBER 14

No man or woman knows
*what perfect love is, until they have
been married a quarter of a century.*

—MARK TWAIN

 JANUARY 19

*The togetherness for which I hope
is one in which the strength in each
of us will complement the
weakness of the other.*

—EDWIN A. ROBINSON

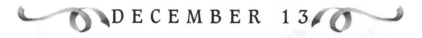

DECEMBER 13

*Let him kiss me with the kisses
of his mouth—for his love is
more delightful than wine.*

—SONG OF SONGS 1:2 NIV

JANUARY 20

We are each a secret to the other.
*To know one another means to feel
mutual affection and confidence,
and to believe in one another.*

—ALBERT SCHWEITZER

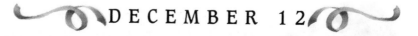
DECEMBER 12

*Love, like a lamp, needs to be fed
out of the oil of another's heart,
or its flame burns low.*

—HENRY WARD BEECHER

JANUARY 21

Your attitude should be the kind
that was shown us by Jesus who...did
not demand and cling to his rights.

—PHILIPPIANS 2:5 TLB

DECEMBER 11

Love is like a mirror. When you love another you become his mirror and he becomes yours.... And reflecting each other's love you see infinity.

—LEO BUSCAGLIA

 JANUARY 22

*It takes years to marry completely
two hearts, even of the most loving.
A happy wedlock is a long falling in love.*

—THEODORE PARKER

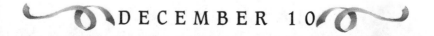

DECEMBER 10

*How beautiful you are, my dearest,
O how beautiful, your eyes are like doves.*

—SONG OF SONGS 1:15 NEB

JANUARY 23

*To be in love, as to see beauty,
is a kind of adoring that turns
the lover away from self.*

—SHELDON VANAUKEN

DECEMBER 9

Love is love's reward.

—JOHN DRYDEN

 JANUARY 24

A happy marriage is like mountain climbing—the climbers are safe only so long as they are tied securely together.

—ROBERT W. BURNS

 DECEMBER 8

*Looking back on all that we've shared
and all that is yet to come, I realize that
nothing life may offer me could make me
happier than a future filled with loving you.*

—ANONYMOUS

JANUARY 25

*F*ew delights can equal the mere presence
of one whom we trust utterly.

—GEORGE MACDONALD

 DECEMBER 7

You have stolen my heart,...my bride,
you have stolen my heart.

—SONG OF SONGS 4:9 NIV

JANUARY 26

*The highest love of all finds
its fulfillment not in what it keeps,
but in what it gives.*

—FATHER ANDREW

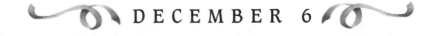 DECEMBER 6

*Seeing eye to eye in marriage often
requires the bigger person to bend a bit.*

—COLLIE

JANUARY 27

*If life has meaning to us at all,
it possesses it because of love.*

—M. M. WEITZ

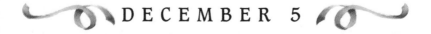

DECEMBER 5

*A woman would rather marry
a poor provider than a poor listener.*

—K. HUBBARD

 JANUARY 28

As the bridegroom rejoiceth over the bride, so shall thy God rejoice over thee.

ISAIAH 62:5 KJV

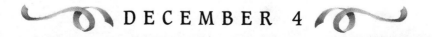

DECEMBER 4

*Many waters cannot quench love;
rivers cannot wash it away.*

—SONG OF SONGS 8:7 NIV

JANUARY 29

The goal in marriage is not to think alike but to think together.

—R. C. DODDS

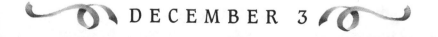

DECEMBER 3

*Who ever strikes at marriage
either by word or act undermines the
foundation of all moral society.*

—JOHANN WOLFGANG VON GOETHE

JANUARY 30

Let me see your face, let me hear your voice;
for your voice is sweet, and your face is lovely.
Arise, my love, my fair one, and come away.

—SONG OF SOLOMON 2:13,14 NRSV

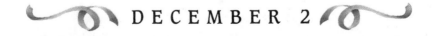 DECEMBER 2

*Marriage is the beautiful blending
of two lives, two loves, two hearts.
It's the wonderful, mystical moment
when a beautiful love story starts.*

—ANONYMOUS

JANUARY 31

Love is a fruit in season at all times and within the reach of every hand.

—MOTHER TERESA

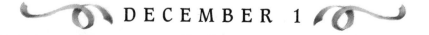

DECEMBER 1

A man leaves his father and mother
and is united to his wife, and
the two become one flesh.

—GENESIS 2:24 NEB

 FEBRUARY 1

The Lord God said, "It is not good for the man to be alone. I will make a helper suitable for him."

—GENESIS 2:18 NIV

NOVEMBER 30

An anniversary says, "Think of the dreams you have weathered together. They are intimate accomplishments."

—CHARLES SWINDOLL

FEBRUARY 2

A kiss is a secret told to the mouth instead of to the ear.

—EDMOND ROSTAND

 NOVEMBER 29

We've grown to be one soul—two parts;
Our lives so intertwined
that when some passion stirs your heart,
I feel the quake in mine.

—GLORIA GAITHER

 FEBRUARY 3

It is never too late to fall in love.

—S. WILSON

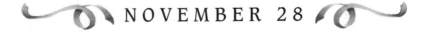

NOVEMBER 28

Find a wife and you find a good thing;
so you will earn the favour of the Lord.

—PROVERB 18:22 NEB

 FEBRUARY 4

The way is long—let us go together.
The way is difficult—let us help each other.
The way is joyful—let us share it.
The way is ours alone—let us go in love.

—ANONYMOUS

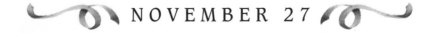 NOVEMBER 27

*A kiss is a rosy dot placed
on the "i" in loving.*

—EDMOND ROSTAND

FEBRUARY 5

*May the love you share be as timeless
as the tides and as deep as the sea.*

—ANONYMOUS

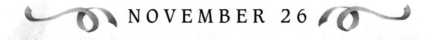 NOVEMBER 26

*A beautiful woman appeals to the eye;
a good woman appeals to the heart.
One is a jewel; the other, a treasure.*

—NAPOLEON

FEBRUARY 6

Charm is deceptive, and beauty is fleeting; but a woman who fears the Lord is to be praised.

—PROVERBS 31:30 NIV

NOVEMBER 25

The heart that loves is always young.

—ANONYMOUS

FEBRUARY 7

Though weary, love is not tired;
Though pressed, it is not straitened;
Though alarmed, it is not confounded.
Love securely passes through all.

—THOMAS À KEMPIS

 NOVEMBER 24

A wife of noble character...
is clothed with strength and dignity;
she can laugh at the days to come.

—PROVERBS 31:10,25 NIV

 FEBRUARY 8

*A gentle heart is tied
with an easy thread.*

—GEORGE HERBERT

 NOVEMBER 23

Love rules without a sword,
Love binds without a cord.

—ANONYMOUS

FEBRUARY 9

*When one loves somebody, everything
is clear—where to go, what to do—
it all takes care of itself.*

—MAXIM GORKI

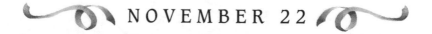 NOVEMBER 22

*Glorify the Lord with me,
and let us praise his name together.*

—PSALM 34:3 NCV

FEBRUARY 10

*W*hither thou goest, I will go;
and where thou lodgest, I will lodge:
thy people shall be my people,
and thy God my God.

—RUTH 1:16 KJV

NOVEMBER 21

Love, and do what you like.

—ST. AUGUSTINE

 FEBRUARY 11

Love is a battle,
Love is a war;
Love is growing up.

—JAMES BALDWIN

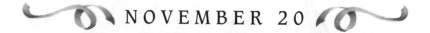

NOVEMBER 20

Respect is what we owe;
Love, what we give.

—P. J. BAILEY

FEBRUARY 12

Love is the greatest refreshment in life.

—PABLO PICASSO

NOVEMBER 19

Many women do noble things,
but you surpass them all.

—PROVERBS 31:29 NIV

FEBRUARY 13

*Depend on the Lord in whatever you do.
Then your plans will succeed.*

—PROVERBS 16:3 NCV

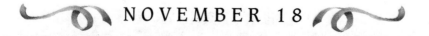 NOVEMBER 18

*You are my friend, my love,
my forever valentine.*

—FLAVIA WEEDN

FEBRUARY 14

*Love is the fusion of two hearts—
the union of two lives—the coming
together of two tributaries.*

—PETER MARSHALL

NOVEMBER 17

*God's grace is the oil
that fills the lamp of love.*

—HENRY WARD BEECHER

FEBRUARY 15

*We can only love what we know
and we can never know completely
what we do not love.*

—ANONYMOUS

 NOVEMBER 16

*Love spends his all,
and still hath store.*

—P. J. BAILEY

FEBRUARY 16

*Humility and reverence
for the Lord will make you both
wise and honored.*

—PROVERBS 15:33 TLB

 NOVEMBER 15

*What we love
we shall grow to resemble.*

—ST. BERNARD OF CLAIRVAUX

FEBRUARY 17

True love is a discipline in which each divines the secret self of the other and refuses to believe in the mere daily self.

—ANONYMOUS

NOVEMBER 14

*Unspoken promise
of a soul's allegiance—this,
All this, and more, ah more!
is in a kiss.*

—M. PHELPS

FEBRUARY 18

*A person who can really love
is not afraid to reveal himself.*

—H. M. LYND

NOVEMBER 13

Harmony is as precious as fragrant anointing oil, as refreshing as dew.

—PSALM 133:1 TLB

FEBRUARY 19

His mouth is sweet to kiss.
I desire him very much.
Yes...this is my lover.
This is my friend.

—SONG OF SONGS 5:16 NCV

 NOVEMBER 12

Where love is, there's no lack.

—R. BROME

FEBRUARY 20

Love is the active concern for the life and growth of that which we love.

—ERICH FROMM

NOVEMBER 11

*Love is a tender plant;
when properly nourished,
it becomes sturdy and enduring.*

—H. B. BROWN

FEBRUARY 21

What do I get from loving you?
Loving.
You.

—JOHN ROGER

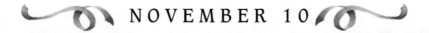 NOVEMBER 10

*Love creates a special world
for two people. Everything within
it is guarded and preserved by
commitment, faithfulness and trust.*

—ANONYMOUS

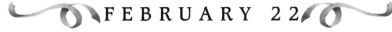

FEBRUARY 22

$\mathcal{B}$ut in the Lord,
*the woman is important to the man,
and the man is important
to the woman.*

—1 CORINTHIANS 11:11 NCV

 NOVEMBER 9

*Love thrives in the face of
all life's hazards, save one—neglect.*

—JOHN DRYDEN

FEBRUARY 23

Love has never known a law
Beyond its own sweet will.

—JOHN GREENLEAF WHITTIER

 NOVEMBER 8

Love is a symbol of eternity.
It wipes out all sense of time.

—DE STAËL

FEBRUARY 24

Marriage is the salt of daily life.
It makes everything just a little bit better.

—DR. JOYCE BROTHERS

 NOVEMBER 7

Then God said to the woman...
"You shall welcome your
husband's affections."

—GENESIS 3:16 TLB

FEBRUARY 25

This is what marriage really means: helping one another to reach the full status of being persons, responsible beings who do not run away from life.

—PAUL TOURNIER

NOVEMBER 6

*Love is always bestowed as a gift—
freely, willingly, and without expectation....
We don't love to be loved; we love to love.*

—LEO BUSCAGLIA

FEBRUARY 26

I will betroth you to me in faithfulness and love, and you will really know me then as you never have before.

—HOSEA 2:20 TLB

NOVEMBER 5

*All of us need more love
than we deserve.*

—ANONYMOUS

FEBRUARY 27

*Loving can cost a lot
but not loving always costs more.*

—M. SHAIN

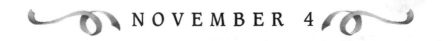 NOVEMBER 4

*Above all else, guard your heart,
for it is the wellspring of life.*

—PROVERBS 4:23 NIV

FEBRUARY 28

*Love is a great thing.
By itself it makes everything
that is heavy light; and it bears
evenly all that is uneven.*

—THOMAS À KEMPIS

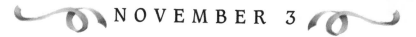

NOVEMBER 3

*The deepest truth blooms only
from the deepest love.*

—HEINRICH HEINE

FEBRUARY 29

*Beloved, if God so loved us,
we also ought to love one another.*

—1 JOHN 4:11 RSV

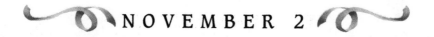

NOVEMBER 2

Love makes all hard hearts gentle.

—GEORGE HERBERT

 MARCH 1

*Love knows no limit to its endurance,
no end to its trust, no fading of its hope;
it can outlast anything. Love still stands
when all else has fallen.*

—ANONYMOUS

 NOVEMBER 1

*While faith makes all things possible,
it is love that makes all things easy.*

—GERARD MANLEY HOPKINS

 MARCH 2

Ay, marriage is the life-long miracle,
The self-begetting wonder, daily fresh.

—CHARLES KINGSLEY

OCTOBER 31

When our relationships are born in the heart of God, they bring out the best in us, for they are nurtured by love.

—DON LESSIN

 MARCH 3

*Remember that you and your wife
are partners in receiving God's blessings.*

—1 PETER 3:7 TLB

OCTOBER 30

Like a lily among thorns
is my darling among the maidens.

—SONG OF SONGS 2:2 NIV

 MARCH 4

One does not fall "in" or "out" of love.
One grows in love.

—LEO BUSCAGLIA

OCTOBER 29

Until I truly loved, I was alone.

—CHARLES E. NORTON

 MARCH 5

*Marriage is a lifelong process
of discovering each other more deeply.*

—INGRID TROBISCH

OCTOBER 28

He who forgives first, wins.

—WILLIAM PENN

 MARCH 6

*Let him have all your worries
and cares, for he is always thinking
about you and watching everything
that concerns you.*

—1 PETER 5:7 TLB

 OCTOBER 27

Two are better than one....
If one falls down, his friend can help
him up.... If two lie down together,
they will keep warm.

—ECCLESIASTES 4:9-11 NIV

 MARCH 7

*Love is often
a fruit of marriage.*

—MOLIÈRE

 OCTOBER 26

Those who love deeply never grow old.

—ARTHUR W. PINERO

 MARCH 8

Love has ever in view the absolute loveliness
of that which it beholds. Where loveliness is
incomplete, it spends itself to make more
lovely, that it may love more.

—GEORGE MACDONALD

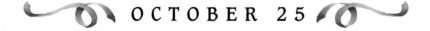

OCTOBER 25

*Love must be learned again and again;
there is no end to it.*

—KATHERINE ANNE PORTER

 MARCH 9

Dawn love is silver,
Wait for the west:
Old love is gold love—
Old love is best.

—K. L. BATES

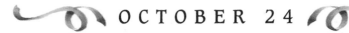 OCTOBER 24

Speaking the truth in love.

—EPHESIANS 4:15 KJV

 MARCH 10

*Husbands,...be considerate
as you live with your wives, and treat
them with respect...so that nothing
will hinder your prayers.*

—1 PETER 3:7 NIV

OCTOBER 23

Let the burden never be so heavy;
love makes it light.

—ROBERT BURTON

 MARCH 11

*Love cannot be bought
except with love.*

—JOHN STEINBECK

 OCTOBER 22

*The course of true love
never did run smooth.*

—SHAKESPEARE

 MARCH 12

Love.

No greater theme can be emphasized.
No stronger message can be proclaimed.
No finer song can be sung.
No better truth can be imagined.

—CHARLES SWINDOLL

 OCTOBER 21

*Be kind and compassionate
to one another, forgiving each other,
just as in Christ God forgave you.*

—EPHESIANS 4:32 NIV

 MARCH 13

*Always be willing to listen
and slow to speak.*

—JAMES 1:19 NCV

OCTOBER 20

Love is indestructible;
Its holy flame forever burneth;
From heaven it came,
To earth returneth.

—ROBERT SOUTHEY

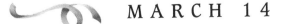 MARCH 14

*Love is an act of endless forgiveness,
a tender look which becomes a habit.*

—PETER USTINOV

OCTOBER 19

*Loving relationships are
a family's best protection against
the challenges of the world.*

—B. WIEBE

 MARCH 15

*Honor your marriage
and its vows, and be pure.*

—HEBREWS 13:4 TLB

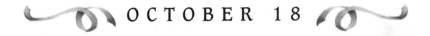

OCTOBER 18

*Be humble and give more honor
to others than to yourselves.*

—PHILIPPIANS 2:3 NCV

 MARCH 16

*Marriages may be made in heaven,
but man is responsible for the
maintenance work.*

—CHANGING TIMES

OCTOBER 17

So long as we love, we serve.

—ROBERT LOUIS STEVENSON

 MARCH 17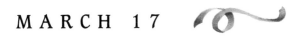

Be kind to one another:
This is the Golden Rule of marriage
and the secret of making love last
through the years.

—RANDOLPH RAY

OCTOBER 16

$\mathscr{T}$he ever-living Christ is here to
bless you. The nearer you keep to Him,
the nearer you will be to one another.

—ARCHBISHOP OF CANTERBURY

 MARCH 18

Let your conversation be always gracious.

—COLOSSIANS 4:6 NEB

 OCTOBER 15

Love is very patient and kind.

—1 CORINTHIANS 13:4 TLB

 MARCH 19

*The true measure of loving...
is to love without measure.*

—ST. BERNARD OF CLAIRVAUX

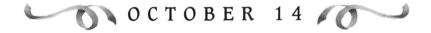 OCTOBER 14

Spring bursts today,
For love is risen
and all the earth's at play.

—CHRISTINA ROSSETTI

 MARCH 20

*To crown all, there must be love,
to bind all together and complete the whole.*

—COLOSSIANS 3:14 NEB

OCTOBER 13

Each kiss a heart-quake—
for a kiss's strength,
I think, it must be reckoned
by its length.

—LORD BYRON

 MARCH 21

To love is to admire with the heart.

—ANONYMOUS

OCTOBER 12

*W*hat therefore God hath joined
together, let not man put asunder.

—MATTHEW 19:6 KJV

 M A R C H 2 2

And when my lips meet thine,
Thy very soul is wedded unto mine.

—H. H. BOYESEN

OCTOBER 11

God, the best maker of all marriages,
Combine your hearts in one.

—SHAKESPEARE

 MARCH 23

Get along with each other,
and forgive each other...because
the Lord forgave you.

—COLOSSIANS 3:13 NCV

 OCTOBER 10

A loving relationship is home for one's soul—
a place to be ourselves and explore our deepest
inner yearnings, hopes, fears, and joys,
without fear of condemnation, rejection,
or being abandoned.

—LEO BUSCAGLIA

 MARCH 24

My true love hath my heart,
and I have his. By just exchange,
one for the other given.

—SIR PHILIP SIDNEY

 OCTOBER 9

Love is not irritable or touchy.

—1 CORINTHIANS 13:5 TLB

 MARCH 25

You should practice tenderhearted mercy and kindness to others.

—COLOSSIANS 3:12 TLB

OCTOBER 8

Not from his head was woman took,
As made her husband to o'er look;
But fashioned for himself a bride;
An equal, taken from his side.

—S. WESLEY

 MARCH 26

Knit your hearts
With an unslipping knot.

—SHAKESPEARE

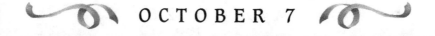

OCTOBER 7

Thou art my life, my love, my heart,
The very eyes of me:
And hast command of every part
To live and die for thee.

—ROBERT HERRICK

 MARCH 27

*Or bid me love,
And I will give a loving heart to thee.
A heart as kind and free
As in the whole world thou canst find.
That heart I'll give to thee.*

—ROBERT HERRICK

OCTOBER 6

*Love is never glad about injustice,
but rejoices whenever truth wins out.*

—1 CORINTHIANS 13:6 TLB

 MARCH 28

Let everyone see that you are unselfish and considerate in all you do.

—PHILIPPIANS 4:5 TLB

OCTOBER 5

*Love feels no burden,
thinks nothing of trouble,
attempts what is above its strength.*

—THOMAS À KEMPIS

 MARCH 29

*Love carries a burden
which is no burden.*

—THOMAS À KEMPIS

 OCTOBER 4

*Beautiful in the eyes of the Lord
are a man and wife who are inseparable.*

—M. S. ECCLES

 MARCH 30

No sky is heavy if the heart is light.

—WINSTON CHURCHILL

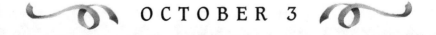

OCTOBER 3

If you love someone you will be loyal to him no matter what the cost.

—1 CORINTHIANS 13:7 TLB

 MARCH 31

My heart is ever at your service.

—SHAKESPEARE

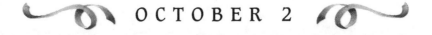 OCTOBER 2

With this ring I thee wed,
With my body I thee worship,
And with all my worldly goods
I thee endow.

—BOOK OF COMMON PRAYER

 APRIL 1

Don't worry about anything;...
pray about everything; tell God your
needs and don't forget to thank
him for his answers.

—PHILIPPIANS 4:6,7 TLB

OCTOBER 1

$\mathcal{O}$ perfect Love,
all human thought transcending,
Lowly we kneel in prayer
before Thy throne.

—D. F. GURNEY

 APRIL 2

Kiss rhymes with bliss
in fact, as well as verse.

—LORD BYRON

SEPTEMBER 30

*Married love burns as fire,
and seeks nothing more than the mate.
It says, "I want only you."*

—MARTIN LUTHER

 APRIL 3

In pleasure's dream, or sorrow's hour,
In crowded hall, or lonely bower,
The business of my soul shall be
Forever to remember thee!

—MOORE

SEPTEMBER 29

If you love someone...
you will always believe in him, always
expect the best of him, and always stand
your ground in defending him.

—1 CORINTHIANS 13:7 TLB

 APRIL 4

Love does not demand its own way.

—1 CORINTHIANS 13:5 TLB

SEPTEMBER 28

*Love softens me, and blows up fires
which pass through my tough heart
and melt the stubborn mass.*

—JOHN DRYDEN

 APRIL 5

*But thou dost make
the very night itself…
brighter than day.*

—HENRY WADSWORTH LONGFELLOW

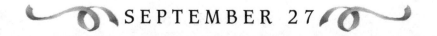

SEPTEMBER 27

Guide us in your truth.
Teach us, our God, our Savior.
We trust you all day long.

—PSALM 25:5 PARAPHRASED

 APRIL 6

*Love...it begins with a moment
that grows richer and brighter...
and becomes a lifetime of joy.*

—ANONYMOUS

SEPTEMBER 26

Not where I breathe,
But where I love,
I live.

—ROBERT SOUTHEY

 APRIL 7

Such a large and sweet fruit is a complete marriage that it needs a long summer to ripen it, and then a long winter to mellow and season it.

—THEODORE PARKER

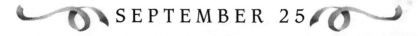

SEPTEMBER 25

*I belong to my lover,
and he desires only me.*

—SONG OF SONGS 7:10 NCV

 APRIL 8

*To love anyone is nothing else than
to wish that person good.*

—THOMAS AQUINAS

SEPTEMBER 24

*Husbands who have the courage
to be tender enjoy marriages that
mellow through the years.*

—B. FRANCIS

 APRIL 9

Tender teacher, comrade, wife,
A fellow-farer true thru life,
Heart-whole and soul-free,
The august Father gave to me.

—ROBERT LOUIS STEVENSON

SEPTEMBER 23

It is love which gives things their value.

—C. CARRETTO

 APRIL 10

May you always be doing those good, kind things which show you are a child of God, for this will bring much praise and glory to the Lord.

—PHILIPPIANS 1:11 TLB

SEPTEMBER 22

*Encourage each other
to build each other up,
just as you are already doing.*

—1 THESSALONIANS 5:11 TLB

 APRIL 11

*The luckiest thing that ever happened
to me was the girl I married.*

—DWIGHT EISENHOWER

SEPTEMBER 21

*The love of a man and a woman
gains immeasurably in power when
placed under divine restraint.*

—ELISABETH ELLIOT

 APRIL 12

*It takes patience to appreciate
domestic bliss.*

—GEORGE SANTAYANA

SEPTEMBER 20

Love is infallible; it has no errors,
for all errors are the want of love.

—WILLIAM LAW

 APRIL 13

Each one of you also must love his wife as he loves himself, and the wife must respect her husband.

—EPHESIANS 5:33 NIV

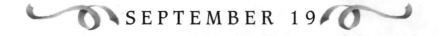

SEPTEMBER 19

My children, we should love people
not only with words and talk, but by
our actions and true caring.

—1 JOHN 3:18 NCV

 APRIL 14

*Love has its source in God, for love
is the very essence of His being.*

—KAY ARTHUR

SEPTEMBER 18

Love makes everything lovely.

—GEORGE MACDONALD

 APRIL 15

Marriage is the most natural state of man and, therefore, the state in which you will find solid happiness.

—BENJAMIN FRANKLIN

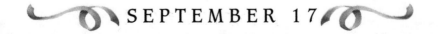

SEPTEMBER 17

Love cures people—both the ones who give it and the ones who receive it.

—KARL MENNINGER

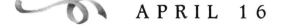 A P R I L 16

*Love is a passion which kindles
honor into noble acts.*

—JOHN DRYDEN

 SEPTEMBER 16

Be subject one to another,
and be clothed with humility.

—1 PETER 5:5 KJV

 APRIL 17

*Keep thy eyes wide open before marriage,
and half shut afterwards.*

—BENJAMIN FRANKLIN

 SEPTEMBER 15

Love does not consist in gazing
at each other but in looking outward
together in the same direction.

—ANTOINE

 APRIL 18

Love is...never jealous or envious.

—1 CORINTHIANS 13:4 TLB

SEPTEMBER 14

Love is the only power that can overcome the self-centeredness that is inherent in being alive.

—ARNOLD TOYNBEE

 APRIL 19

Life's lasting joy comes in erasing the boundary line between "mine" and "yours."

—ANONYMOUS

SEPTEMBER 13

Can two walk together,
except they be agreed?

—AMOS 3:3 KJV

 APRIL 20

*Kind words can be easy to speak,
but their echoes are truly endless.*

—MOTHER TERESA

SEPTEMBER 12

*There is no limit to the power
of a good woman.*

—R. H. BENSON

 APRIL 21

The heart hath its own memory, like the mind,
And in it are enshrined
The precious keepsakes, into which is wrought
The giver's loving thought.

—HENRY WADSWORTH LONGFELLOW

SEPTEMBER 11

*Marriage is our last,
best chance to grow up.*

—J. BARTH

 APRIL 22

Be imitators of God...
and live a life of love.

—EPHESIANS 5:1,2 NIV

SEPTEMBER 10

Serve each other with love.

—GALATIANS 5:13 NCV

 APRIL 23

The heart is wiser than the intellect.

—J. G. HOLLAND

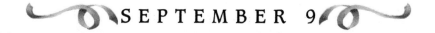

SEPTEMBER 9

Success in marriage is more than finding the right person: it is a matter of being the right person.

—RABBI BRICKNER

 APRIL 24

Love lights more fires
Than hate extinguishes.

—ELLA WHEELER WILCOX

 SEPTEMBER 8

*The state of marriage is
one that requires more virtue and
constancy than any other; it is a
perpetual exercise of mortification.*

—FRANCIS DESALES

 APRIL 25

*D*o not be interested only in
your own life, but be interested in the
lives of others. In your lives you must
think and act like Christ Jesus.

—PHILIPPIANS 2:4-5 NCV

SEPTEMBER 7

The winter is past; the rains are over and gone. Flowers appear on the earth; the season of singing has come.... Arise, my darling; my beautiful one, come with me.

—SONG OF SONGS 2:11-13 NIV

 APRIL 26

*Love is always in the mood
of believing in miracles.*

—JOHN COWPER POWYS

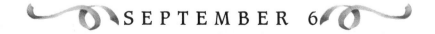

SEPTEMBER 6

A successful marriage demands a divorce: a divorce from your own self-love.

—P. FROST

 APRIL 27

Love scarce is love that never knows
The sweetness of forgiving.

—JOHN GREENLEAF WHITTIER

SEPTEMBER 5

*A happy marriage is a union
of two good forgivers.*

—ANONYMOUS

 APRIL 28

But the fruit of the Spirit is love, joy, peace, patience, kindness, goodness, faithfulness, gentleness, and self-control.

—GALATIANS 5:22,23 NIV

SEPTEMBER 4

*Be humble and gentle.
Be patient with each other,
making allowance for each other's
faults because of your love.*

—EPHESIANS 4:2 TLB

 APRIL 29

Love is not getting, but giving;
it is goodness and honor
and peace and pure living.

—HENRY VAN DYKE

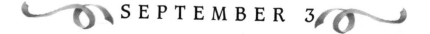

SEPTEMBER 3

*Have a heart that never hardens,
and a temper that never tires,
and a touch that never hurts.*

—CHARLES DICKENS

 APRIL 30

*Love is the strange bewilderment
which overtakes one person
on account of another person.*

—JAMES THURBER

SEPTEMBER 2

When my hair has all turned gray,
Will you kiss me then and say
That you love me in December
As you do in May?

—JAMES J. WALKER

 M A Y   1

Love is...never boastful or proud.

—1 CORINTHIANS 13:4 TLB

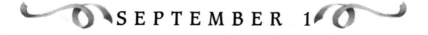

SEPTEMBER 1

You are joined together with peace through the Spirit, so make every effort to continue together in this way.

—EPHESIANS 4:3 NCV

 MAY 2

Love is not only something you feel.
It is something you do.

—DAVID WILKERSON

AUGUST 31

A good wife and health
are a man's best wealth.

—H. G. BOHN

 MAY 3

*There is no remedy for love
but to love more.*

—HENRY DAVID THOREAU

 AUGUST 30

*Try praising your spouse,
even if they do get frightened at first.*

—W. A. "BILLY" SUNDAY

 M A Y   4

Kisses kept are wasted;
Love is to be tasted.

—E. V. COOKE

 AUGUST 29

Say only what is good and helpful...
and what will give...a blessing.

—EPHESIANS 4:29 TLB

 MAY 5

In your anger do not sin.
Do not let the sun go down
while you are still angry.

—EPHESIANS 4:26 NIV

 AUGUST 28

*In a kiss, two spirits meet,
mingle, and become one.*

—ST. AELRED

 MAY 6

The hours I spent with thee, dear heart,
Are as a string of pearls to me;
I count them over, every one apart.

—R. C. ROGERS

AUGUST 27

*How great is God's goodness
to have given you to me
to love for a lifetime.*

—ANONYMOUS

 MAY 7

*We loved with a love
that was more than love—
A love that the winged seraphs
of heaven coveted.*

—EDGAR ALLAN POE

AUGUST 26

Confess your faults one to another,
and pray one for another.

—JAMES 5:16 KJV

 MAY 8

Be of one mind, live in peace.
And the God of love and peace
will be with you.

—2 CORINTHIANS 13:11 NIV

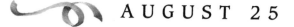 AUGUST 25

The greatest gift bestowed upon humans is the gift of giving love between man and woman.

—M. M. WEITZ

 MAY 9

They that love beyond the world cannot be separated by it. Death cannot kill what never dies.

—WILLIAM PENN

AUGUST 24

*He who is filled with love
is filled with God himself.*

—ST. AUGUSTINE

 MAY 10

Grow old along with me!
The best is yet to be,
The last of life for which
the first was made.

—ROBERT BROWNING

 AUGUST 23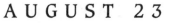

Above all, keep your love for each other at full strength, because love cancels innumerable sins.

—1 PETER 4:8 NEB

 MAY 11

*Moments shared with you are
refreshing streams of heaven's light.*

—ANONYMOUS

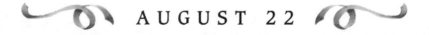 AUGUST 22

Love seeketh not itself to please,
Nor for itself hath any care,
But for another gives its ease,
And builds a Heaven in Hell's despair.

—WILLIAM BLAKE

 M A Y   1 2

Big problems frequently strengthen marriages.... It's the little things... we seldom even consider that cut away at the heart of a home.

—CHARLES SWINDOLL

 AUGUST 21

It is the purest sign that we love someone if we choose to spend time idly in their presence when we could be doing something more constructive.

—S. CASSIDY

 MAY 13

In marriage reverence is important...
A steady awareness in each that the
other has a kinship with God.

—FULTON J. SHEEN

 AUGUST 20

*Be good servants and use
your gifts to serve each other.*

—1 PETER 4:10 PARAPHRASED

 MAY 14

*Love keeps the cold out better than
a cloak. It serves for food and raiment.*

—HENRY WADSWORTH LONGFELLOW

 AUGUST 19

*Love does not allow the lover
to belong anymore to himself,
but he belongs only to the Beloved.*

—ST. DIONYSIUS

 MAY 15

The Lord has done great things
for us, and we are filled with joy.

—PSALM 126:3 NIV

AUGUST 18

If mountains can be moved by faith,
is there less power in love?

—FREDERICK W. FABER

 MAY 16

Love...will have the whole and not a part.

—HENRY WADSWORTH LONGFELLOW

 AUGUST 17

Learn as you go along
what pleases the Lord.

—EPHESIANS 5:10 TLB

 MAY 17

*A loving relationship is a wanting
to celebrate, communicate, and know
another's heart and soul.*

—LEO BUSCAGLIA

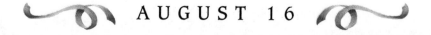

AUGUST 16

*Love is the child of freedom,
never that of domination.*

—ERICH FROMM

 MAY 18

*Love is...never haughty
or selfish or rude.*

—1 CORINTHIANS 13:5 TLB

AUGUST 15

*$\mathscr{A}$s a result of a kiss, there arises
in the mind a wonderful feeling of delight
that awakens and binds together
the love of them that kiss.*

—ST. AELRED

 MAY 19

Perhaps true love can best be recognized by the fact that it thrives under circumstances which would blast anything else into small pieces.

—E. HAVEMANN

AUGUST 14

*D*on't act thoughtlessly,
but try to find out and do whatever
the Lord wants you to.

—EPHESIANS 5:17 TLB

 MAY 20

*In the last analysis, love is only
the reflection of a person's own
worthiness from other persons.*

—RALPH WALDO EMERSON

 AUGUST 13

How blessed I am that I can walk beside you, lean upon you, and live within the warmth of your love.

—ROY LESSIN

 MAY 21

Life's short and we never have enough time for the hearts of those who travel the way with us. O, be swift to love! Make haste to be kind.

—HENRI FRÉDÉRICK AMIEL

AUGUST 12

An instant of pure love is more precious than all other good works.

—ST. JOHN OF THE CROSS

 MAY 22

*Love...does not hold grudges
and will hardly even notice when
others do it wrong.*

—1 CORINTHIANS 13:5 TLB

 A U G U S T   1 1

Being rooted and grounded in love, we are able to comprehend the breadth and length, and depth, and height, and to know the love of Christ.

—EPHESIANS 3:17,18 PARAPHRASED

 MAY 23

*There is something so indescribably
sweet and satisfying in the knowledge
that a husband or wife has forgiven
the other freely, and from the heart.*

—HENRIK IBSEN

AUGUST 10

*Wheresoever a man seeketh his own
there he falleth from love.*

—THOMAS À KEMPIS

 MAY 24

Love and a cough cannot be hid.

—GEORGE HERBERT

 AUGUST 9

Love is the only force capable of transforming an enemy into a friend.

—MARTIN LUTHER KING

 MAY 25

May the Lord make your love increase and overflow for each other and for everyone else.

—1 THESSALONIANS 3:12 NIV

 AUGUST 8

*Be subject to one another
out of reverence for Christ.*

—EPHESIANS 5:21 NEB

 MAY 26

Love rules the court, the camp, the grove,
And men below, and saints above;
For love is heaven and heaven is love.

—SIR WALTER SCOTT

 AUGUST 7

To love and to be loved
the wise would give...
All that for which alone
the unwise live.

—WALTER S. LANDOR

 MAY 27

No cord nor cable can so forcibly draw, or hold so fast, as love can do with a twined thread.

—ROBERT BURTON

 AUGUST 6

*To know ourselves loved
is to have the depths of our own
capacity to love opened up.*

—J. MAIN

 MAY 28

*Love each other deeply
with all your heart.*

—1 PETER 1:22 NCV

 AUGUST 5

Wives, be subject to your husbands as to the Lord; husbands, love your wives, as Christ also loved the church and gave himself up for it.

—EPHESIANS 5:22,25 NEB

 MAY 29

Love is the only game that is not called on account of darkness.

—ANONYMOUS

 AUGUST 4

To be able to say how much love,
is to love but little.

—PETRARCH

 MAY 30

Love cuts away the clouds with strokes
Adept as surgeon's knife,
And leaves the trusting heart aglow
With glorious love of life!

—GLORIA GAITHER

 AUGUST 3

Do whatever arouses you most to love.

—ST. TERESA

 MAY 31

Love builds up.

—1 CORINTHIANS 8:1 NCV

 AUGUST 2

Love each other...and take delight in honoring each other.

—ROMANS 12:10 TLB

 JUNE 1

Kissing is a means of getting two people so close together that they can't see anything wrong with each other.

—G. YASENAK

 AUGUST 1

*A husband is really listening
when he can understand every word
his wife isn't saying.*

—ANONYMOUS

 JUNE 2

Two souls with but a single thought,
Two hearts that beat as one.

—BELLINGHAUSEN

 JULY 31

*A wife is to thank God
her husband has faults; a husband
without faults is a dangerous observer.*

—LORD HALIFAX

 JUNE 3

So let us try to do what makes peace and helps one another.

—ROMANS 14:19 NCV

 JULY 30

Live together in peace with each other.

—ROMANS 12:16 NCV

 JUNE 4

*There is more pleasure in loving
than in being loved.*

—THOMAS FULLER

 JULY 29

*I have found a paradox
that if I love until it hurts, then there
is no hurt, but only more love.*

—MOTHER TERESA

 J U N E 5

My bounty is as boundless as the sea,
My love as deep; the more I give to thee
The more I have, for both are infinite.

—SHAKESPEARE

 JULY 28

To love as Jesus loves...
when all is said and done...is the only
thing we have to learn, for it is perfection.

—R. VOILLAUME

 J U N E 6

Love does no wrong to anyone....
It is the only law you need.

—ROMANS 13:10 TLB

 JULY 27

*Be glad for all God is planning
for you. Be patient in trouble,
and prayerful always.*

—ROMANS 12:12 TLB

 JUNE 7

For thy sweet love rememb'red
such wealth brings
That then I scorn to change
my state with Kings.

—SHAKESPEARE

 JULY 26

*There is no more lovely, friendly,
or charming relationship, communion,
or company than a good marriage.*

—MARTIN LUTHER

 JUNE 8

Come live with me and be my love,
And we will all the pleasures prove.

—CHRISTOPHER MARLOWE

 JULY 25

*A good husband and father
is really praying all the time.*

—V. MCNABB

 JUNE 9

Let no debt remain outstanding,
except the continuing debt
to love one another.

—ROMANS 13:8 RSV

 J U L Y   2 4

*Oh, how delightful you are;
how pleasant, O love, for utter delight!*

—SONG OF SOLOMON 7:6 TLB

 J U N E   1 0

God in His ample love embraces our love
with...a sort of tenderness, and we must
tread the Way to Him hand in hand.

—SHELDON VANAUKEN

 JULY 23

Let mutual fidelity continue until death. This may be considered as the summary of the highest law for husband and wife.

—ANCIENT LAW

 JUNE 11

To see her is to love her,
And love but her for ever,
For nature made her what she is,
And ne'er made another!

—ROBERT BURNS

 JULY 22

*I want to help you to grow
as beautiful as God meant you to be
when He thought of you first.*

—GEORGE MACDONALD

 JUNE 12

*O love! O fire! Once he drew
With one long kiss my whole soul thro'
My lips, as sunlight drinketh dew.*

—TENNYSON

 JULY 21

*Don't store up treasures here on earth
where they can erode away or may be
stolen. Store them in heaven where
they will never lose their value.*

—MATTHEW 6:19,20 TLB

 J U N E   1 3

*The great acts of love are done
by those who are habitually performing
small acts of kindness.*

—ANONYMOUS

 JULY 20

The well of life is love.

—JOHANNES TAULER

 JUNE 14

*Let men beware of causing women
to weep; God counts their tears.*

—HEBREW PROVERB

 JULY 19

Love is not love,
Which alters when it alteration finds.

—SHAKESPEARE

 JUNE 15

To love means to decide to live with an equal partner, and to subordinate oneself to the formation of a new subject, a "we."

—F. KUNKEL

 JULY 18

*So don't be anxious about tomorrow.
God will take care of your tomorrow too.
Live one day at a time.*

—MATTHEW 6:34 TLB

 JUNE 16

Let love be genuine.

—ROMANS 12:9 RSV

 JULY 17

*Love is the sweet, tender,
melting nature of God flowing
into the creature, making the creature
most like unto himself.*

—I. PENNINGTON

 JUNE 17

*True love is but a humble,
low-born thing.... It is a thing to
walk with hand in hand, through the
everydayness of this workaday world.*

—JAMES R. LOWELL

 JULY 16

*Love is a desire of the whole being
to be united to some other being.*

—SAMUEL T. COLERIDGE

 JUNE 18

Too many married people expect their partner to give that which only God can give, namely, an eternal ecstasy.

—FULTON J. SHEEN

 JULY 15

*Do for others what you want them
to do for you.*

—MATTHEW 7:12 TLB

 JUNE 19

This is my commandment, that you love one another as I have loved you.

—JOHN 15:12 RSV

 JULY 14

*There is nothing holier,
in this life of ours, than the first
consciousness of love.*

—HENRY WADSWORTH LONGFELLOW

 JUNE 20

Marriage is that relation between a man and woman in which the independence is equal, the dependence mutual, and the obligation reciprocal.

—LOUIS K. ANSPACHER

 JULY 13

*Love is the celestial breathing
of the atmosphere of paradise.*

—VICTOR HUGO

 JUNE 21

Shine! Shine! Shine!
Pour down your warmth, great sun!
While we bask, we two together.

—WALT WHITMAN

 JULY 12

Hatred stirs up trouble.
But love forgives all wrongs.

—PROVERBS 10:12 NCV

 JUNE 22

What is a kiss? Why this,
as some approve:
The sure sweet cement, glue,
and lime of love.

—ROBERT HERRICK

 JULY 11

*There is no soul that does
not respond to love.*

—MAURICE MAETERLINCK

 JUNE 23

*Your attitude must be like my own,
for I, the Messiah, did not come to be
served, but to serve, and to give my
life as a ransom for many.*

—MATTHEW 20:28 TLB

 JULY 10

Love is the expansion of two natures in such fashion that each includes the other, each is enriched by the other.

—FELIX ADLER

 JUNE 24

Adam could not be happy
even in Paradise without Eve.

–J. LUBBOCK

 JULY 9

*Your strong love for each other
will prove to the world that
you are my disciples.*

—JOHN 13:35 TLB

 JUNE 25

*Between a man and his wife
nothing ought to rule but love.*

—WILLIAM PENN

 JULY 8

Love builds memories that endure,
to be treasured up as hints of
what shall be hereafter.

—B. JARRET

 J U N E   2 6

*Love creates a special world
for two people. Everything about it is
enriched and endeared by kindness,
gentleness and care.*

—ANONYMOUS

 J U L Y 7

*When love is real love,
a miracle is produced.*

—ERNEST DIMNET

 JUNE 27

*W*here the flesh is one,
one also is the spirit.

—TERTULLIAN

 JULY 6

Let love be your greatest aim.

—1 CORINTHIANS 14:1 TLB

 J U N E   2 8

I will never lose the wonder of you.
I will forever enjoy the beauty of you.
I will always treasure the memory of you.
You are my love, my gift!

—ROY LESSIN

 JULY 5

*Human love would never have
the power it has were it not rooted
in an express image of God.*

—J. MOUROUX

 JUNE 29

If two of you on earth agree about something and pray for it, it will be done for you by my Father in heaven.

—MATTHEW 18:19 NCV

 JULY 4

*Love is a mutual self-giving
which ends in self-recovery.*

—FULTON J. SHEEN

 JUNE 30

*We can only love each other because
God has loved us first—and we can
love each other with the same love.*

—A. CARRE

 J U L Y 3

And whatever you do,
do it with kindness and love.

—1 CORINTHIANS 16:14 TLB

 JULY 1

*Physical love is total intimacy.
It is the sign that the lovers have
nothing to refuse each other, that
they belong wholly to each other.*

—J. LECLERCQ

 JULY 2